NEW AND  POEMS

NEW AND SELECTED POEMS

RICHARD EBERHART

North Star Line Poetry Series
Edited by Jay Parini

For Bob

Karen

with joy & to Ithaca

Richard Eberhart

NORTH STAR LINE/NEW YORK

First Blue Moon Edition 1990
First Printing 1990

ISBN 0-929654-95-1 (Hardcover)
ISBN 0-929654-91-9 (Paperbound)

Manufactured in the United States of America

A North Star Line Book
Published by Blue Moon Books, Inc.
61 Fourth Avenue
New York, New York 10003

Acknowledgments

Many of these poems previously appeared in COLLECTED POEMS by Richard Eberhart. Copyright 1987. Oxford University Press. Previously published poems appeared first in the following collections: A BRAVERY OF EARTH, READING THE SPIRIT, SONG AND IDEA, POEMS NEW AND SELECTED, BURR OAKS, SELECTED POEMS, UNDERCLIFF, GREAT PRAISES, COLLECTED POEMS 1930–1960, THE QUARRY, SELECTED POEMS 1930–1965, SHIFTS OF BEINGS, FIELDS OF GRACE, WAYS OF LIGHT, THE LONG REACH, FOUR POEMS, FLORIDA POEMS, THE BREAD LOAF ANTHOLOGY, COLLECTED POEMS, 1930–1986.

NEW AND SELECTED POEMS: 1930–1990

by RICHARD EBERHART

Edited, with a Preface by Jay Parini

Contents

PREFACE

Richard Eberhart has always gone his own way as a poet, belonging to no school, resisting any label of contemporaneity. Still, his work has been influenced in fruitful ways by a wide range of poets from Blake and Shelley to Frost, Stevens, and William Carlos Williams. While his poems have been amply recognized by the conventional awards and prizes, including the Pulitzer Prize for Poetry and the Bollingen Award, Eberhart has never attracted the kind of readership he deserves.

This neglect has something to do with the astonishing quantity and relatively uneven quality of his output. Eberhart's *Collected Poems: 1930-1986* contains over four hundred densely printed pages—a spectacle that may easily frighten off all but specialists and partisans. And then there is the unevenness: so many of his poems are unrealized or abstract, self-consciously naive in their deportment or oracular in ways that trouble post-modern readers, who have grown up on understatement, concreteness, and the kind of superficial sophistication taught in writing schools. But Eberhart, like Robert Penn Warren and other immensely productive writers, tends to work through the process of revision in public; consequently, he has printed too many poems that stand up badly to his best work—a situation which occludes his originality and achievement.

What future generations will realize, I suspect, is that Richard Eberhart is among the finest poets of this century. Critics with as different tastes as Harold Bloom, Cleanth Brooks, F.R. Leavis and Christopher Ricks have recognized his visionary intensity and lyric gifts, but the message has not filtered down to the larger reading public. Many younger poets still have never read anything by Eberhart except, perhaps, "The Groundhog," which remains among the most anthologized poems of this century, or "The Fury of Aerial Bombardment," perhaps the best poem to come out of World War II.

Eberhart's poetry is tuned like none other. It is by turns bold and gentle, fierce and loving. A poem such as "Sea-Hawk," for instance, has all the primal energy and linguistic muscle of Ted Hughes, but it remains quite unknown. "Opulence" is another small masterpiece, a poem of almost breathless calm and grandeur. The same can be said for endless other poems in his *Collected*, though few readers have got to them.

A late Romantic of the purest kind, this unusual poet has always taken it upon himself to praise what remains mysterious, to fight back at death, and to acknowledge decay with a certain sorrow but no final bitterness. A sense of life's fragility governs his work right from the beginning, with "Cover Me Over." It continues through the present. In his latest poems, especially, an autumnal serenity permeates the language—as in "A Loon Call," as fine a lyric as has been published in recent years. My hope is that this *New and Selected Poems** will attract the kind of sympathetic readership it deserves.

JAY PARINI

*The poems appear in chronological order; the eleven poems prior to the last poem, "A Loon Call," are published here for the first time.

FOR A LAMB

I saw on the slant hill a putrid lamb,
Propped with daisies. The sleep looked deep,
The face nudged in the green pillow
But the guts were out for crows to eat.

Where's the lamb? whose tender plaint
Said all for the mute breezes.
Say he's in the wind somewhere,
Say, there's a lamb in the daisies.

THE GROUNDHOG

In June, amid the golden fields,
I saw a groundhog lying dead.
Dead lay he; my senses shook,
And mind outshot our naked frailty.
There lowly in the vigorous summer
His form began its senseless change,
And made my senses waver dim
Seeing nature ferocious in him.
Inspecting close his maggots' might
And seething cauldron of his being,
Half with loathing, half with a strange love,
I poked him with an angry stick.
The fever arose, became a flame
And Vigour circumscribed the skies,
Immense energy in the sun,
And through my frame a sunless trembling.
My stick had done nor good nor harm.
Then stood I silent in the day
Watching the object, as before;
And kept my reverence for knowledge
Trying for control, to be still,
To quell the passion of the blood;
Until I had bent down on my knees
Praying for joy in the sight of decay.
And so I left; and I returned
In Autumn strict of eye, to see
The sap gone out of the groundhog,
But the bony sodden hulk remained.
But the year had lost its meaning,
And in intellectual chains
I lost both love and loathing,
Mured up in the wall of wisdom.

Another summer took the fields again
Massive and burning, full of life,
But when I chanced upon the spot
There was only a little hair left,
And bones bleaching in the sunlight
Beautiful as architecture;
I watched them like a geometer,
And cut a walking stick from a birch.
It has been three years, now.
There is no sign of the groundhog.
I stood there in the whirling summer,
My hand capped a withered heart,
And thought of China and of Greece,
Of Alexander in his tent;
Of Montaigne in his tower,
Of Saint Theresa in her wild lament.

'IF I COULD ONLY LIVE AT THE PITCH THAT IS NEAR MADNESS'

If I could only live at the pitch that is near madness
When everything is as it was in my childhood
Violent, vivid, and of infinite possibility:
That the sun and the moon broke over my head.

Then I cast time out of the trees and fields,
Then I stood immaculate in the Ego;
Then I eyed the world with all delight,
Reality was the perfection of my sight.

And time has big handles on the hands,
Fields and trees a way of being themselves.
I saw battalions of the race of mankind
Standing stolid, demanding a moral answer.

I gave the moral answer and I died
And into a realm of complexity came
Where nothing is possible but necessity
And the truth wailing there like a red babe.

'COVER ME OVER'

Cover me over, clover;
Cover me over, grass.
The mellow day is over.
And there is night to pass.

Green arms about my head,
Green fingers on my hands.
Earth has no quieter bed
In all her quiet lands.

NEW HAMPSHIRE, FEBRUARY

Nature had made them hide in crevices,
Two wasps so cold they looked like bark.
Why I do not know, but I took them
And I put them
In a metal pan, both day and dark.

Like God touching his finger to Adam
I felt, and thought of Michaelangelo,
For whenever I breathed on them,
The slightest breath,
They leaped, and preened as if to go.

My breath controlled them always quite.
More sensitive than electric sparks
They came into life
Or they withdrew to ice,
While I watched, suspending remarks.

Then one in a blind career got out,
And fell to the kitchen floor. I
Crushed him with my cold ski boot,
By accident. The other
Had not the wit to try or die.

And so the other is still my pet.
The moral of this is plain.
But I will shirk it.
You will not like it. And
God does not live to explain.

THE FURY OF AERIAL BOMBARDMENT

You would think the fury of aerial bombardment
Would rouse God to relent; the infinite spaces
Are still silent. He looks on shock-pried faces.
History, even, does not know what is meant.

You would feel that after so many centuries
God would give man to repent; yet he can kill
As Cain could, but with multitudinous will,
No farther advanced than in his ancient furies.

Was man made stupid to see his own stupidity?
Is God by definition indifferent, beyond us all?
Is the eternal truth man's fighting soul
Wherein the Beast ravens in its own avidity?

Of Van Wettering I speak, and Averill,
Names on a list, whose faces I do not recall
But they are gone to early death, who late in school
Distinguished the belt feed lever from the belt holding paw

AT NIGHT

In the dust are my father's beautiful hands,
In the dust are my mother's eyes.
Here by the shore of the ocean standing,
Watching: still I do not understand.

Love flows over me, around me,
Here at night by the sea, by the sovereign sea.

Gone is that bone-hoard of strength;
Gone her gentle motion laughing, walking.

Is it not strange that disease and death
Should rest, by the undulant sea?

And I stare, rich with gifts, alone,

Feeling from the sea those terrene presences,
My father's hands, my mother's eyes.

THE HORSE CHESTNUT TREE

Boys in sporadic but tenacious droves
Come with sticks, as certainly as Autumn,
To assault the great horse chestnut tree.

There is a law governs their lawlessness.
Desire is in them for a shining amulet
And the best are those that are highest up.

They will not pick them easily from the ground.
With shrill arms they fling to the higher branches,
To hurry the work of nature for their pleasure.

I have seen them trooping down the street
Their pockets stuffed with chestnuts shucked, unshucked.
It is only evening keeps them from their wish.

Sometimes I run out in a kind of rage
To chase the boys away: I catch an arm,
Maybe, and laugh to think of being the lawgiver.

I was once such a young sprout myself
And fingered in my pocket the prize and trophy.
But still I moralize upon the day

And see that we, outlaws on God's property,
Fling out imagination beyond the skies,
Wishing a tangible good from the unknown.

And likewise death will drive us from the scene
With the great flowering world unbroken yet,
Which we held in idea, a little handful.

SEALS, TERNS, TIME

The seals at play off Western Isle
In the loose flowing of the summer tide
And burden of our strange estate—

Resting on the oar and lolling on the sea,
I saw their curious images,
Hypnotic, sympathetic eyes

As the deep elapses of the soul.
O ancient blood, O blurred kind forms
That rise and peer from elemental water:

I loll upon the oar, I think upon the day,
Drawn by strong, by the animal soft bonds
Back to a dim pre-history;

While off the point of Jagged Light
In hundreds, gracefully, the fork-tailed terns
Draw swift esprits across the sky.

Their aspirations dip in mine,
The quick order of their changing spirit,
More freedom than the eye can see.

Resting lightly on the oarlocks,
Pondering, and balanced on the sea,
A gauze and spindrift of the world,

I am in compulsion hid and thwarted,
Pulled back in the mammal water,
Enticed to the release of the sky.

THE CANCER CELLS

Today I saw a picture of the cancer cells,
Sinister shapes with menacing attitudes.
They had outgrown their test-tube and advanced,
Sinister shapes with menacing attitudes,
Into a world beyond, a virulent laughing gang.
They looked like art itself, like the artist's mind,
Powerful shaker, and the taker of new forms.
Some are revulsed to see these spiky shapes;
It is the world of the future too come to.
Nothing could be more vivid than their language,
Lethal, sparkling and irregular stars,
The murderous design of the universe,
The hectic dance of the passionate cancer cells.
O just phenomena to the calculating eye,
Originals of imagination. I flew
With them in a piled exuberance of time,
My own malignance in their racy, beautiful gestures
Quick and lean: and in their riot too
I saw the stance of the artist's make,
The fixed form in the massive fluxion.

I think Leonardo would have in his disinterest
Enjoyed them precisely with a sharp pencil.

GREAT PRAISES

Great praises of the summer come
With the flushed hot air
Burdening the branches.

Great praises are in the air!
For such a heat as this
We have sweated out our lives toward death.

I used to hate the summer ardour
In all my intellectual pride,
But now I love the very order

That brushed me fast aside,
And rides upon the air of the world
With insolent, supernal splendour.

SEA-HAWK

The six-foot nest of the sea-hawk,
Almost inaccessible,
Surveys from the headland the lonely, the violent waters.

I have driven him off,
Somewhat foolhardily,
And look into the fierce eye of the offspring.

It is an eye of fire,
An eye of icy crystal,
A threat of ancient purity,

Power of an immense reserve,
An agate-well of purpose,
Life before man, and maybe after.

How many centuries of sight
In this piercing, inhuman perfection
Stretch the gaze off the rocky promontory,

To make the mind exult
At the eye of a sea-hawk,
A blaze of grandeur, permanence of the impersonal.

ON A SQUIRREL CROSSING THE ROAD
IN AUTUMN, IN NEW ENGLAND

It is what he does not know,
Crossing the road under the elm trees,
About the mechanism of my car,
About the Commonwealth of Massachusetts,
About Mozart, India, Arcturus,

That wins my praise. I engage
At once in whirling squirrel-praise.

He obeys the orders of nature
Without knowing them.
It is what he does not know
That makes him beautiful.
Such a knot of little purposeful nature!

I who can see him as he cannot see himself
Repose in the ignorance that is his blessing.

It is what man does not know of God
Composes the visible poem of the world.

> . . . Just missed him!

ONLY IN THE DREAM

Only in the dream that is like sleep
When time has taken the measure of live things
By stark origination
Is mankind redeemed.

Only in the melancholy of the music
Of the midnight within the blood
Comes the fulfilment
After faring years.

Only in the balance of dark tenderness
When everything is seen in its purity
Do we penetrate
The myth of mankind.

Only in the mastery of love
Is anything known of the world,
Death put aside
With pure intent.

Only in the long wastes of loss
Comes the mystical touch on the brow
That triumph grow,
Insatiable, again.

OFF SPECTACLE ISLAND

Seals and porpoises present
A vivid bestiary
Delightful and odd against the mariner's chart.

The sea bells do not locate them,
Nor lights, nor the starred ledges;
We are unprotected from their lyricism.

They play in the blue bay, in day,
Or whoosh under the midnight moonlight;
We go from point to point where we are going.

I would rather see them playing,
I would rather hear them course
Than reach for Folly from Pride's Light.

IN AFTER TIME

In after time, when all this dream
Becomes pure dream, and roughest years
Lie down among the tender grass,
And spring up sentient upon the meadow;

In that after time of great-born Aprils,
Beyond a century of tatters and of malice,
When love has thrown out fear and madness
The eyes will see the sun as wonder.

In after time, when rage and chaos
Lose their sovereign force, new dream
Will lift the shining life to spirit
And mate the make of man to merit.

Then shall holy summers come; then laughter
God-like shake upon a dewy morning;
Then fullness grow, big with purpose,
And man shall know again his richness.

THE SUPREME AUTHORITY OF THE IMAGINATION

Life longs to a perfection it never achieves.
Voices from the grave, with a wry grimace, whisper,
"We were never satisfied, we tried toward perfection,
We were undone. It is nothing to be a cipher."

Life breeds its joy in the incomplete.
A flag flying in a moment of the Atlantic
Lifts the spirit, lavishes a serene sign,
As halest happiness is death to the frantic.

Aesthetic purity stays with the rose bud.
Desire is renewed in every lover's glance,
The ununderstandable is always understood,
It is the shyest by the wall most wish to dance.

It is the grace to imagine the unimaginable
Elevates man to an angelic state
In which he may dwell, formidable and alone,
In the simplicity of the truly great.

It is the supreme authority of the imagination
Brings a frothed brightness to the human scene,
Bottle of industry, looking glossy-fine,
The blood-tip breezy and the anchor twined.

A rose of Spring seen with an even eye
Never betrayed the seer; he leaps the sight
And stands within ineluctable dominions,
Saved in some haven of a sheer delight.

THE OAK

Some sway for long and then decline.
There are those, a very few,
Whose rings are golden, hard, and just,
Like a solid oak all through.

Each year builds on another truth,
A suffering, a joy increased in gold.
You cannot see, viewing the edifice,
Whether it is young or old.

Some have it in them to keep close
To nature, her mysterious part,
Seeming strange to be so natural,
Nature married to perfected art.

Flesh will ponder its dark blame.
Mind will never mate the true.
But the whole being will rejoice,
Like a solid oak all through.

OSPREYS IN CRY

When I heard the call of the osprey,
The wild cries of the ospreys
Breasting the wind high above
The cliff, held static
On updraft over the ocean,
Piercing with ancient, piercing eyes
The far ocean deep

I felt a fleshed exultance
For the fierce, untamed beauty
Of these sea-birds, sea-hawks,
Wild creatures of the air,
Magnificent riders
Of the wind's crests, plummeters
Straight down for prey

Caught under water in talons
Triumphant as life,
The huge birds struggling up
Shaking heavy water off
And powerfully taking the air
With fish in talons head first;

I felt a staggering sense
Of the victor and of the doomed,
Of being one and the other,
Of being both at one time,
I was the seer
And I was revealed.

EQUIVALENCE OF GNATS AND MICE

As a pillar of gnats, moving up and down
In June air, toward opulent sunset,
Weaving themselves in and out, up and down,

As diaphanous as visual belief,
In scintillant imagination, is slightest dancing,
Weaves a major harmony of nature;

As tiny field mice are saved from the sickle
By a lean seventy-year-old scyther in Maine
Who brings them in, saying, "They have enemies enough";

Who are hand-fed by a dropper on milk and water,
Hoping the small creatures will survive and thrive,
Slight event against the history of justice,

It is necessary to hail delicacy
Whenever encountered in nature or man;
No disharmony come near this poem.

SEA BURIAL FROM THE CRUISER *REVE*

She is now water and air,
Who was earth and fire.

Reve we throttled down
Between Blake's Point and Western Isle,

Then, oh, then, at the last hour,
The first hour of her new inheritance,

We strewed her ashes over the waters,
We gave her the bright sinking

Of unimaginable aftermaths,
We followed her dispersed spirit

As children with a careless flick of wrist
Cast on the surface of the sea

New-cut flowers. Deeper down,
In the heavy blue of the water,

Slowly the white mass of her reduced bones
Waved, as a flag, from the enclosing depths.

She is now water and air,
Who was earth and fire.

WINTER KILL

Word traps catch big bears in silence.
They hunt the woods for years in freedom,
Keeping the counsels of the bees and snows.
Then, once unwary, a foot is caught in a trap.
The big black mountain comes atumble down.

His picture is put in the local paper.
The expressionless hunter stands in sullen pride;
A small son touches the nose of the brute.
The gun rests easy by the icy carcass;
People come to stare at the winter kill.

I would have him noble on the mountain side,
Roaming and treading, untrapped by man.
Man kills him only half for meaning,
Half out of thoughtlessness. The steaks
Are passed around as tokens to the neighbors.

Word traps catch big bears another way
When the meaning is total. The way a poem prinks
Into the heart from a forest hill
Is to have it in words, but never to have it.
Which is to say it is elusive still.

THE ILLUSION OF ETERNITY

Things of this world
In pure afternoons of gold,
And splendor of October,
Radiant air, still trees,
Give the illusion of eternity.

As if there were no suffering,
No ancient heart-ache of the being,
No tortures of the soul,
No struggle with mortality,
But changelessness, eternity.

A leaf falls here and there.
There are small birds a-chirp,
A chipmunk on a pine tree,
No cloud in the sky,
October afternoon, gold rarity.

Through the transparent air
Time is a kind of singing
In the inner being,
Acceptable singing,
Giving the illusion of eternity.

OPULENCE

Nothing is so magnificent
As the sun descending,
Copernicus-gold over the horizon,
With birds singing in the pine trees
When it is rich summer, when June
Has on her iris finery
And peony-bright, hesitates good-bye.

Nothing is so magnificent
As the full mind, stored with summers,
With age approaching,
The sun standing over the horizon,
Wonders yet unknown, love not refusing,
The world all a visionary
Guess, unspent clarity.

TO THE FIELD MICE

Come small creatures of low estate, friskily moving,
Make sally along the stone escarpment, toward evening.
The stones do not move in their millennial inability,
But you move, bright-eyed creatures of the height of summer,
Seem to scamper on errands of urgency,

You show yourselves in flashes and dart back in the rocks,
You look out with alert eyes, small in the large, still rocks,
Instinct with life in the short time of your devotion,
I behold you and love you as opposed to the rocks, dashers
For food or whatever you are doing unknown to me observing,
I am god-like to you, you do not know that I exist,

See I sit still, I watch, I observe your cautious walkings
As the late afternoon changes to early evening,
I wish you well whatever may be your purpose.
Above you stand the flowers, above them stands the sky.
It is the height of summer, I watch the grand occasion
And give you, white-footed field mice, my fidelity.

THE HAYSTACK

In memory I see a youth
And a girl looking into each other's eyes,
In the surge and height of their life principle,
Which they do not understand.

On a northern lake in a rowboat
They catch a glittering fish, slight
Catch, they think nothing of it.
Grace is theirs, youth's insolence.

Back at the house an old man
Drools and cannot speak a word.
They look at each other. They drool.
They fall together behind the gray-green haystack.

ON RETURNING TO A LAKE IN SPRING

When the new frogs in their exuberant arrivals
By hundreds raised their voices in lusty croaks
As I walked up to my knees in reeds among them,
Wading through the wet strong forces of present nature
As if I felt for the first time a divination
So powerful as to shake my frame beyond words,

And only the small frogs could speak harsh articulation
Of the pure force racking them to ecstasy,
When I strode like a god among the small,
The bright movers, the true, walking in triumph
As a king of the frogs, glad to be among them,
As they touched my legs as I moved along,

I remarked their destiny, their birth and death
As one sure of mine, the minimal existence, here in
The great opening of the world again, sure as I was
Of the summer life, in full sunlight, of frogs and men,
I was equally sure of the fall of the year, winter,
The razoring sleet, and locking ice and snow.

I returned to the picnic on the hill exulting.
In our party a young woman moving in her youth
Seemed to jump at the glory of the springtime;
Nevertheless she did not speak of the spring peepers.
A month later, in a southern bog, she slit her throat.

THE SWALLOWS RETURN

For five years the swallows did not build
In the treehouse near the door facing the sea.
I felt their absence as furtive and wordless.
They were put out of mind because they had to be.

Then they came again, two males attending one female,
Skimming in the late afternoon gracefully, ardent
And free in quick glides and arcs, catching flies on the wing,
Feeding their young in the house safely pent.

It was mid-summer, the time of high July,
Their return as mysterious as their former leaving.
They presented the spectacle of orderly nature,
Their lives to some deep purpose cleaving?

At night there was clamor. When morning came
The ground under the house was littered with feathers.
None knows who was the predator, but death
Is available to birds as to man in all weathers.

GNAT ON MY PAPER

He has two antennae,
They search back and forth,
Left and right, up and down.

He has four feet,
He is exploring what I write now.

This is a living being,
Is this a living poem?

His life is a quarter of an inch.
I could crack him any moment now.

Now I see he has two more feet,
Almost too delicate to examine.

He is still sitting on this paper,
An inch away from An.

Does he know who I am,
Does he know the importance of man?

He does not know or sense me,
His antennae are still sensing.

I wonder if he knows it is June,
The world in its sensual height?

How absurd to think
That he never thought of Plato.

He is satisfied to sit on this paper,
For some reason he has not flown away.

Small creature, gnat on my paper,
Too slight to be given a thought,

I salute you as the evanescent,
I play with you in my depth.

What, still here? Still evanescent?
You are my truth, that vanishes.

Now I put down this paper,
He has flown into the infinite.
He could not say it.

VERMONT IDYLL

These are the days of yellow and red
Thrown up across a far field,
October's eyeball-striking glory,
A day that imitates the summer,
The leaves are falling, will come winter.

You lie upon the grass, the sun is hot,
Your skin is moist, you think of summer,
But when you stand and walk a cool
Cleanliness of the lengthening day
Reaches a white winter in the bones.

And then the silence of this time
Is opened by an engine's oncome
Coming slowly with growing invasion,
Changing meditation,
Until goes past, across, the manure spreader.

The red and yellow sentinels stand by.
The lurcher machine, immigrant, throws out
Its rich burden over unplowed grass,
A secret ritual or rebirth,
The hand of man applying the levers.

Only a moment without man's agency
It seemed a timeless perfection
Was one with consciousness,
A stasis like a dreaming mind
Between summer and winter.

Nearby, a car rotting among thistles
Had jagged glass, teeth of broken windows.
In the back, a ruined cushion with a hole
In the center. A discarded plow rusted too,
As time was stalking.

EMBLEM

A great snowy owl
Sat on a cupola
Looking wise,
But undoubtedly thinking of mice
Who might be down under the barn
To come out to be devoured.

He had flown in from the far north,
So large and commanding a bird
Hundreds came daily to gape.
His head swiveled,
His eyes were astonishing,
His silence complete.

ADAM CAST FORTH
Translated from Jorge Luis Borges

Was there a garden or was the garden a dream?
I ask myself, slowly in the evening light,
Almost for consolation, without delight,
If that past was real or if it only seems
Real to me now in misery, an illusion?
   No more than a magical show
   Of a god I do not know
But dreamed, and that Paradise, vague now, delusion?
   But I know that Paradise will be
   Even if it does not exist for me.
The warring incest of Cains and Abels is the tough earth's way
Of punishing me. Yet it is a good thing to have known of
Happiness and to have touched love,
The living garden, even if only for a day.

UNDERCLIFF EVENING

I feel illimitable essence,
As if I could express everything
Known to man. This omnipotence
Is a gift of nature in radiant acclaim

That I can know a secret of being.
This instant a parti-colored butterfly
Flew across my sight, real as evanescence,
Startled me in its non-verbal reality.

Bandied butterfly, severed spectacle,
Coming to consciousness for an instant.
You are a messenger of supernal power.
You escape the words of poetry.

I try to put you in words, you are evidence
Of a dream of insubstantiality,
A moment of perfection in the dream of time,
You vanish forever, I shall not know you

But as a feeling of illimitable essence,
When the world, despite error and chaos,
Announces gripped summits, elects to show
Mysteries beyond our tongue, shafts of light.

I did not ask you to come to me,
I did not ask you to fly by my face,
But you erase my heavy thoughts.
You bring me into lightness and grace.

SNOW CASCADES

Snow cascades from the tall pines,
Large powder puffs
Puff down in soft lunges,

Descending to earth,
Subdued incidence,
A sort of soul of January.

They do not have words for it.
If they are wordless,
So, finally, are we.

It is as if they would say
What we say,
I mean what I say by being.

VISION THROUGH TIMOTHY

Vision through timothy
Is different from vision as if it were clear.
Looking at reality, looking at the sea
Through timothy, occludes partially the view.
It is meshes of extreme nature,
You cannot see through nature's extremity.

You see partially. This is the reality of vision,
To see partially through nature's extremity.
Veils were drawn over our eyes
When we were born, or else
We would have knowledge of eternity
Upon our eyesight, yet we see

Only man in his adversity, man incomplete.
We set up great universities
To see man complete, yet his nature
Eludes us in our strenuous studies,
We cannot determine the reality,
We are caught in the nature of perplexity.

Love leaps in the nature
Of vision through timothy.
Timothy comes lifting in July,
July is a high time of the year,
If I were sitting here
In October, timothy would disappear

And I should be more bland, more austere.
I would think I would see
The world as it would inevitably appear,
But would I be more human,
In a vision so incontestable,
Than looking through timothy to see the sea?

GNATS

A society of gnats
Hangs on a beam of light
Near the ground, toward evening.

Then they rise up
And hang in the air,
Animatedly bunched.

What is their meaning?
I cannot guess their meaning
They are so ephemeral.

Nature makes them come and go,
As it does us. We
Amass our own society,

And I cannot guess our meaning,
Although I have tried for fifty years,
Twisting and turning.

A SNOWFALL

As the snow falls I brush it away
With a delicate broom so as not to use a shovel.
Every hour I go out to the long walk,
Conquer the new swirls and pile as if persistence
Were a virtue to keep up with nature.
If I did nothing I would be snowed in.
Some slumberous thinkers think this the best, January.
Let three feet fall, stay indoors, go to sleep,
Luxuriate in sleep like the groundhogs and gray squirrels.

There is something in me to test nature,
To disallow it the archaic predominance,
And if the skies blanket us entirely
With a silence so soft as to be wholly winsome,
(This beguilement of something beyond the human)
I have enough in me to give affront
And take my thin broom against the thick snowflakes
As a schoolmaster who would tell the children
What to do when they are getting sleepy and lazy.

I now make my predicament equal to nature's.
I have the power, although it is timed and limited,
To assert my order against the order of nature.
The snowplows begin to take away the snow,
Flashing big lights in the middle of the night.
They, corporate, have the same idea that I have,
Individualist, not to let nature better us,
But to take this softness and this plenitude
As aesthetic, and control it as it falls.

LEARNING FROM NATURE

While I was
Sitting on the porch, involved in air,
A small bird
Whisked across low,
Four inches from the floor,
Struck a glass door,
A rectangular pane,
With his bill head-on.

He stood dazed
While I looked on amazed,
The silence ponderable.
I wondered
How hurt he was,
Startled
By aerial reality
Piercing contemplation.

Plato was present,
Sophocles, Shakespeare,
Boehme was looking on,
And so was Blake,
Perhaps Dostoevski in a fit
And my friend Angelus Silesius
In the air.
They were interrupted.

The bird suddenly flew
Off into the darkening afternoon.
He did not say how he was.
He was stopped, and he went on.
It taught me acceptance
Of irrationality,
For if he or we could see better
We would know, but we have to go on.

THE ANGELS

Some angels were standing on the ground
Unable to fly, their wings extended upward.

They kept this stance and pose year after year.
They were made of marble, unable to be human.

These creatures dazzled the ambient Florida sunshine,
Stood immaculate on the ground and never moved.

They looked like perfection, to be eyed askanse
Driving by year after year. Nobody would buy them.

They kept their residence near the lake,
A fisherman came by with big ruddy looks,

Went to the lake and took out a boat.
Green slime and blue water and white sky

Were all in motion when hook and mouth met,
The thrashing resplendent as the man hauled in

A big bright color of life for breakfast, and kept
Fishing all day in the belief of muscle and tone.

The white marble angels were always there, though,
Nobody would buy them, they could not move,

They were perfect and viewed life without expression.
When you passed them you looked but could not think a
    word.

I never forgot them they were so unexpected,
Breath-taking, out of this world, caught in it.

A decade does nothing to them. Nobody would
Buy them. Their marble wings never got off the ground.

They saw me age as I came by another year,
Took out a boat, went on the orange and weedy water

And caught the fish struggling to gasp for air
With no hope, giving his life for my breakfast,

Muscle and tone, while the angels were standing useless,
Unviolated, unable to fly, I thought to buy one

But what would I do with a stiff, marble, non-creature
So resolutely sub and super human, so final,

So far away from my desires and aspirations,
No suffering, no pain and joy, nothing for breakfast.

VELVET ROCKS

A fern coming up shyly
Beside a stone
On a spring day
In May

Pervades the silence
With
A deeper silence
Branching out.

If anything is perfect
The green fern
In May light
Presents itself.

Ramifying, still,
Open, air-touched,
Centuries
Grow delicate.

GOING

The comfortable craggy slope
You go up through knotted roots.
There is a long spell of walking
With little or no talking.

It is a long climb you are making,
A severe journey you are taking,
Under a canopy of twisted trees
Through which you can see the summer sea.

The sea is there in the distance,
You are aware of its existence
As you climb to the goal on the hill,
Something you can do if you will.

It has been done many times before,
Constricted road to an open door.
You brought what you had in your heart
Long before the arduous start.

Some came heavily, some came lightly,
Some have insight, some have no sight,
Some have nothing left to tell
After they have heard the warning bell.

A descent down the moss and rock face
Was necessary from that high place
Down into doubts, uncertainties
In a world of depths of mysteries.

DOG DAYS

A group of homo sapiens all weeping
Stand around the grave of a dog
Half way up the mountain. The earth
Was so hard it took shovels and picks
Half an hour to dig a shallow hole.

We put a heavy stone on top of the grave
To keep one dog from eating another.

A year later there was no sign of the grave.
If you walk up the ferny path you wouldn't know.

If you walk to the top you can pick blueberries,
Look beyond green islands to open blue ocean.

OLD TREE BY THE PENOBSCOT

There is an old pine tree facing Penobscot Bay,
On the bank above the tide,
Like a predecessor. Its fate
Will be that of its forebear.
I watched the former tree ten years
While it faced the surge of the sea.

Whelmings of the tide, line storms
Buffeted the root system of the pine
Twenty feet above the tide.
I watched the changes of the seasons,
Each year returning assessed
Somber change, a kind of stalwart declination.

As children grew up the pine tree grew down,
Threw down its length in defiant slowness,
Until one summer it was almost horizontal.
Even then, with jags of dead branches, it clung
To life, until further summers dipped it down
Until it lay a dry myth along the shore.

There is something ominous in the new tree
Erect on the high bank, at the very edge,
The sea's hands pulling out earth from the roots,
Slowly displacing a system of boulders,
As I watch through soft afternoons.
The tides have slowly taken the children away.

Then this new tree, about to begin to fall
Through subtle gradations of the strength of years,
Took on the force of a grisly apparition,
My memory was forced down to defeat,
My riches gone, my corpse on the beach,
Dry bones, dry branches, I too a myth of time.

MOMENT OF EQUILIBRIUM AMONG
THE ISLANDS

The sea repeats itself in light flourishes,
The southwest breeze-up of the midday
Is a lavish presentiment of possible danger,
Coves beckon as waves attack the prow
And slip past in stubby frenzies of loss.
Then we dare the open ocean; the green swells
We ride over with thorough, lordly motion,
Lovers of wind, sun, and the world-turn horizon,
And seek a new island, with a small spit of sand.
The anchor holds; we climb through contorted woods
Up boulders to an old granite quarry, whose
Dark, green, still, fresh water refutes the ocean.
It is the moment of looking down to still water
From massed granite blocks pleases the soul
With the hardness and fantasy of the world,
Before we must try again the gripping buoyancy
Of the salt sea, whose profound depths
Appear only to the imagination, while eyes
Survey the fresh roads the vessel walks
In triumph of buoyancy, delicacy, and strength,
As a philosopher continuing in the essential.
Then standing to the westward-closing sun
As the wind dies and waves grovel to stillness,
We reach at nightfall the landfall buoy of home.

THE WAY IT IS

Death is so much greater than life
Although we think life is greater than death,
We have to believe it as we live each day.

We do not think of the millions of dead,
Only of the sum of our living friends,
We do not think that time is today.

Beautiful bodies die as certainly as ugly ones.

Our groundhog lives in a hole under the house,
Comes up now and then to show us his suppleness.

JAMES LAUGHLIN

I thought your life was different,
You gave yourself to others, publisher
Who lived to perfect others, flowerily,
Ever renewing the establishment.

Days and months and decades passed,
You were known as a gift to others,
Admired for sanctities of taste and judgment,
As if you had no secret self,

But now your secret self comes out,
You have accreted and secreted poetry
Of love, of love enmeshed with the ancients
Redeeming the world with purity, pure insight,

Your poems are universal, in time, beyond time,
Texture of radiance, flesh and spirit at one time.

HISTORY AND MYSTERY

What is the meaning of existence
If not resistance?

Man has resisted
And persisted

From the cave man up to now
Through millennia somehow.

Some were born hale, some defective,
The process not elective.

Some were once cannibals,
We were always social animals.

How do you account for disparity
With any sense of clarity?

Keats died young, Titian died old,
Some men are sly, some men are bold.

Fixed in our fate on life's tree
Some gain from religion, some from philosophy.

Some are put down or soon sundered,
Others are hale at one hundred.

Man has overpopulated the planet
With John and Jean, Priscilla and Janet.

For all of mankind's persistence, his light
Shines awhile before exacting night.

Trust religion, and trust philosophy
As to what mankind can be, or see.

And if thinking hurts and falls, skip
Over heavy thoughts and announce the comic

But think, almost with every breath
Not about the great mystery of death

But about another, life-dream mystery,
The long life-stream love between you and me.

JUNE 22

If you were a tree you would have no words,
How could you say what you have heard?

It is the longest day of the year.
Is the coming shortest day something to fear?

Sumptuousness is now, toward evening's richness.
There is no word that will rhyme with richness.

A long moment of nature's silence
Blots out any idea of violence.

The time is rich with moveless tress and flowers.
The thought about it is uniquely ours.

We fit into the present as if it were eternity
When it is only the longest day of the year we see.

Full summer is here with lavish insistence,
Our history due to our two-legged persistence.

THE IMMORTAL PICTURE

I want that picture, the perfect view
Of vessels outside our house riding easy,
Great ocean eventuated by islands,
A spectacle of order, harmony, and control

When we know everything is changeful and mortal,
We know the immortal picture is false,
The perfect view will not last,
Change comes on, good turns to bad,
Evil lurks in every picture of man,
Even though we have a good view for Christmas.

The beautiful body decays, the
Beautiful mind is destroyed, the
Great and powerful go to death,

The times change, the poem ends,
The poem ends because heartbreak
Overcomes human beings
Because they cannot control the world.
After twelfth night
We threw the Christmas tree over the cliff.

CHART INDENT

Ile Au Haut is way down there in the distance,
Given a particular kind of day, and if
You are not afraid of the ocean, have daring,
A stout boat and a stout heart

You might sail from here due South,
Pass Eagle Island Light, go into open
Ocean and make for Stonington, if plucky
Continue south to the high island.

Long before getting to Roaring Bull Ledge
Facing the open Atlantic, this
Open enough, you might find a small opening in
The chart and map of the watery world

And there find safe harbor, secure your vessel,
Cast anchor in a safe place, be warned by a native
Not to come far in, the out tide will strand you,
The sea is even treacherous in here, be careful.

You count on the treachery of the sea as endless,
You will haunt her, but you know that every year
She claims lives indifferently, you to be sagacious
And always try to outwit her. Duck in to Duck Harbor,

Sleep snug in sleek harbor, and when dawn comes
Awake to be going out into the ocean
As ancestors have done since time began
And hope you will make safe landfall.

THE BODY AND THE BOOK

Here is my body (points to chest)
And here is my book (holds book out with right arm),
Which is more real?

The body wrote the book,
The book will outlast the body,
Which is more real?

When I was seventeen, very physical,
I had a deep sense of the soul,
Not physical, but metaphysical.

When I knew immediate reality
How I relished life! Yet knew immediately
There is something beyond immediate reality.

If we lived only in the immediate
We would have no sense of values
Which we try to learn and assess all our lives.

I knew that words were a secret, words
Were divinations of a power beyond today.
My body is limited, words can take in all of life.

Here is my body, here is my book.
My book could not write my body,
My body had to write my book.

Which is more real? My body
Without which no book. Or my book
Taking from my body universal secrets?

In this strange, deep kind of dualism
There is a deep, strange kind of unity,
Both are real, the mortal, the immortal.

INSTABILITY

The plates are moving the Himalayas higher,
Southern California is slowly moving north,
The plates are unscalding new islands off
Iceland, lava is running fast in Hawaii.

The plates take millions of years to move
As they separate Africa from South America.
After a meal our plates are moving off,
They seem stable in the churning, hot dishwasher.

THE HOP-TOAD

The hop-toad jumped away, missing the blade,
When Betty was mowing the garden.
She instinctively said, I beg your pardon.

HOW IT IS

Then the eighty-year-old lady with a sparkle,
A Cambridge lady, hearing of the latest
Suicide, said to her friend, turning off
TV for tea, "Well, my dear, doesn't it seem
A little like going where you haven't been invited?"

ALL OF US

Fortified by a piece of paper
The spirit rages in me inconsolable
But what shall I write on the paper?

Shall I say life is magnificent,
All have known moments of magnificence,
Because a moment was magnificent?

Shall I say life is inordinately brief,
Because Mozart lived only thirty-five years
Or that Chatterton lived not two decades?

Shall I say that grief is heavier, more durable
Than happiness, and will never be outlived,
And some sufferings cannot be put into words?

Shall I say that Julia Gray, in open casket yesterday,
who lived to be ninety-one, knew joy and sorrow,
Is not a mystery to existence, like all of us?

Like all of us we are pulled by forces
Greater than we could control, or evaluate.
Time was our enemy who seemed to be our friend,

Fate was our history, to be and not to be.
We were a grain of order in a sea of chance,
Rose and thorn, spirit and matter, life and death.

A LOON CALL

Rowing between Pond and Western Islands
As the tide was coming in
Creating, for so long, two barred islands,
At the end of August, fall nip in the air,
I sensed something beyond me,
Everywhere I felt it in my flesh
As I beheld the sea and sky, the day,
The wordless immanence of the eternal,
And as I was rowing backward
To see directly where I was going,
Harmonious in the freedom of the oars.
A solitary loon cry locked the waters.

Barbaric, indivisible, replete with rack,
Somewhere off where seals were on half-tide rocks,
A loon's cry from beyond the human
Shook my sense to wordlessness.

Perfect cry, ununderstandable essence
Of sound from aeons ago, a shriek,
Strange, palpable, ebullient, wavering,
A cry that I cannot understand.
Praise to the cry that I cannot understand.